DUCKS AND GEESE

CHUCK HAGNER

photographs by TOM VEZO

STACKPOLE
BOOKS

Copyright © 2006 by Stackpole Books

Published by
STACKPOLE BOOKS
5067 Ritter Road
Mechanicsburg, PA 17055
www.stackpolebooks.com

All rights reserved, including the right to reproduce this book or portions thereof in any form or by any means, electronic or mechanical, including photocopying, recording, or by any information storage and retrieval system, without permission in writing from the publisher. All inquiries should be addressed to Stackpole Books, 5067 Ritter Road, Mechanicsburg, PA 17055.

Printed in China

10 9 8 7 6 5 4 3 2 1

First edition

Cover photo of Wood Duck by Tom Vezo
Cover design by Wendy Reynolds
Additional photos provided by Tony Mercieca, Richard Crossley/VIREO, Jari Peltomaki/VIREO, Arthur Morris/VIREO, Sam Fried/VIREO, Morten Strange/VIREO, and Gerrit Vyn/VIREO, as indicated

Library of Congress Cataloging-in-Publication Data

Hagner, Chuck.
   Guide to ducks and geese / Chuck Hagner ; photographs by Tom Vezo. —
1st ed.
     p. cm.
   ISBN-13: 978-0-8117-3344-1
   1. Ducks—Identification. 2. Geese—Identification. I. Title.

   QL696.A52H325 2006
   598.4'1—dc22
                        2006012165

CONTENTS

3 LOONS, GREBES, AND OTHER WATERBIRDS

4 GEESE

DABBLING DUCKS

A helpful way to categorize ducks is by the way they feed. Dabbling ducks lower their heads, necks, and chests into the water while tipping their tail feathers up above the water's surface to feed on plant material, and occasionally small animals. They dive, but very infrequently. Sometimes called puddle ducks, dabbling ducks are usually found in shallow water: streams or ponds or along the edges of rivers and lakes. Because they can get airborne straight out of the water without a running start, they often prefer small pockets of water shielded by surrounding vegetation. Most dabblers are comfortable walking on dry land.

Mallard

Anas platyrhynchos

female

Easily the most familiar, abundant, and widely distributed duck in North America. Stocky and heavy-looking in the air, Mallards are found just about anywhere there is water to swim in.

Adult males are instantly recognizable. They have a large dark green head, a heavy yellow bill about as long as the head is wide, and a chestnut-brown breast. A thin white necklace separates the head and breast. The flanks and wings are pale gray, and the rump and undertail coverts (the small feathers that cover the longer main tail feathers) are black. The tail is two-toned: The outermost tail feathers are white, while those in the center are black and, unique among ducks, noticeably curly.

at left: male Mallard

Female Mallards lack the males' color and curly tail feathers. They are mottled brown all over. A prominent dark line extends from their bill through the eye. Females could be mistaken for American Black Ducks but for their bills: The Mallard's is orange, and its center is black. The black duck's bill is olive on females and greenish yellow on males, but never orange.

The speculum—the colored patch of feathers on the wings of many dabbling ducks—offers another point of distinction. Iridescent violet-blue, it resembles the patch on the back, or trailing, edge of the American Black Duck's wing but is framed top and bottom with bold white bars.

domestic Mallard

© RICHARD CROSSLEY / VIREO

Mallard x American Black Duck hybrid

Mallards interbreed often with American Black Ducks. If you come across a duck whose plumage combines features of both species, you may be looking at a hybrid. Hybrids are recorded frequently in the Northeast. Domestic Mallards, also quite common, are splotched with varying amounts of black and white, creating a piebald appearance.

LOOK FOR a metallic green head, a chestnut-brown breast, black curly tail feathers, and a violet-blue speculum.

American Black Duck

Anas rubripes

male

The American Black Duck is a large dabbling duck and one of the darkest in North America. From tail to breast, it is uniformly blackish brown. Its face is gray-brown, distinguished only by a dark crown and a thin, dark eye stripe. Black ducks do have white feathers that line the lower surface of their wings and contrast sharply with the duck's dark body, but they can be seen only when the bird flies. Otherwise, they remain hidden from view. Even the American Black Duck's iridescent bluish purple speculum looks dark. It resembles the violet-blue patch on the trailing edge of the Mallard's wing but is bordered in black. The Mallard's speculum is framed top and bottom with white bars.

Adult male and female American Black Ducks look similar. To distinguish one from the other, check the color of their bills: The male's is greenish yellow; the female's is olive.

LOOK FOR a large, blackish brown duck with white wing linings, visible in flight.

Mottled Duck

Anas fulvigula

adults

The Mottled Duck is a relative of both the American Black Duck and the Mallard, and it shares a strong family resemblance to each. The overall shape of all three birds is similar, and (except for the male Mallard) each has a dark body and a noticeably lighter head marked with a crown stripe and an eye stripe.

Mottled Ducks have warm brown edges on their body feathers, buff-brown heads, and pale crowns, so they appear lighter in overall tone than American Black Ducks. Moreover, their speculum is iridescent blue-green; on the black duck, it is bluish purple. Nonetheless, these two species are nearly impossible to distinguish when viewed in flight or from afar. Happily, for the most part, Mottled Ducks stay in discrete parts of the continent. They are year-round residents of southern Florida and the Gulf coast of Alabama, Louisiana, Texas, and northern Mexico, but they hardly ever are found outside these areas.

If geography doesn't help, tell Mottled Ducks from female Mallards by their overall tone. Mottled Ducks are darker: Their tail is uniformly dark, they lack the bold white bars that frame the Mallard's speculum, and their bill is either bright yellow (in males) or dull yellow (in females).

LOOK FOR blackish brown body feathers with warm brown edges and an iridescent blue-green speculum without white edges.

Gadwall

Anas strepera

male

The Gadwall is a plain-looking, medium-size duck whose best field mark is a general lack of field marks. Males may show a bit of chestnut on the upper wings but otherwise wear a refined, uniform gray. Even their bill is slate gray. Black feathers above and below the tail give the Gadwall a debonair, two-toned appearance: gray on top and the sides and black behind.

You will find Gadwalls in ponds and marshes throughout the north-central United States, most often while they are dabbling—foraging on underwater stems and leaves. They do this without submerging completely. Rather, like other dabblers, they lever their tails up into the air and tip their heads, necks, and most, but not all, of their bodies beneath the water's surface.

Female Gadwalls are mottled brown, so they look little like males and much like other female dabbling ducks, especially Mallards, but their bill is distinctive. Look for a gray center stripe and orange-yellow sides. And study the upper surface of their wings: Male and female Gadwalls alike have distinctive bright white panels on the trailing edges. Obvious on birds in flight, the patches are harder to see but usually still visible when the duck is swimming. No other dabbling duck has similar white wing patches.

LOOK FOR a mostly gray duck with a black rump and, especially in flight, bright white patches on the wings.

female

Northern Pintail

Anas acuta

male

Elegant Northern Pintails are abundant in the West; over half of the species' North American population migrates through California. Pintails have long, narrow wings, long necks, and small heads, and they often fly in line formation. When they fly, watch for a thin white border on the trailing edge of their wings adjacent to the body.

Male pintails in breeding plumage wear stately attire. Their head is the color of chocolate, their breast and underparts are white, their flanks and back are gray. Two black central tail feathers, the inspiration for the duck's name, extend far beyond an otherwise gray tail. (The Long-tailed Duck, a species found on the open ocean, is the only other North American duck with a tail anything like it. Location easily distinguishes the two: Pintails favor ponds and marshes.) Look closely at the male pintail's neck

female

for another telling field mark: On either side, a narrow white stripe runs up from the chest to the back of the head. The male's bill is black with bluish gray stripes on the sides.

Female pintails possess a pointed tail but lack the male's greatly elongated tail feathers. They have a buff-brown body; a plain-looking, buff head; and a dark gray bill. No other female dabbling duck has a neck so long and thin and a face so plain.

LOOK FOR a slender duck with a long tail, brown head, and long neck with white stripes on either side.

American Wigeon

Anas americana

male

The American Wigeon breeds primarily north of the United States–Canada border, in northwestern North America, but can be found in winter in large numbers in the Pacific Northwest, the Central Valley of California, the high plains of Texas and New Mexico, South Texas, along the Gulf coast, and in the Mid-Atlantic region. Though a dabbling duck, it often forages with American Coots and various diving ducks. It is also sometimes found grazing in upland agricultural areas.

Like the rarer Eurasian Wigeon, adult male American Wigeons have a white-bordered black patch under the tail, but their flanks and breast are rusty and their back and wings are pinkish brown. These features are gray on the Eurasian Wigeon. Most distinctive, the American Wigeon's head is not one color but three: Its neck and cheeks are gray, a broad green streak extends from the eye to the back of the head, and a white stripe runs from the bill to the crown. The stripe—the source of the wigeon's common name Baldpate—stands out even when seen from a distance.

Female Eurasian and American Wigeons are near look-alikes. The best way to distinguish the two species is by comparing their axillars, the feathers in their "wingpits." On Eurasian Wigeons, the axillars are speckled with dark gray. On American Wigeons, they are pure white.

LOOK FOR black under the tail bordered by white, rusty flanks and breast, and a gray head with a green eye patch and white crown stripe.

female

Eurasian Wigeon

Anas penelope

male

© JARI PELTOMAKI/VIREO

Handsome, long-tailed Eurasian Wigeons breed in Europe and Asia, not North America, but vagrants have been recorded from Alaska to California, usually in winter and almost always in flocks of their similar-looking North American cousin, the American Wigeon.

Study adult males from tail to head, looking for sharply defined patches of color: Eurasian Wigeons have black under the tail bordered by a narrow white panel, then pale gray flanks and wings, a pinkish brown chest, and, finally, a rich chestnut head. Look for a smallish dull blue bill with a black hook at the tip (known as the nail) and a streak of buttery yellow on the forehead and crown. When males stretch or take to the air, watch for a panel of bright white on the upper surface of the wings and, on the trailing edge adjacent to the body, a dark green speculum.

Female Eurasian and American Wigeons are near look-alikes. Both wear mottled brown plumage. The best way to distinguish the two species is by comparing their axillars, the feathers located in the birds' "wingpits." On American Wigeons, they are pure white, while on Eurasian Wigeons, they are speckled with dark gray.

LOOK FOR black under the tail bordered by white, pale gray flanks and wings, a pinkish brown chest, and a chestnut head.

© A. MORRIS/VIREO

female

Northern Shoveler

Anas clypeata

male

The most distinctive feature of the Northern Shoveler is its bill, which is very long, shovel-shaped, and unique among North American ducks. It is recognizable even when the bird is viewed from a distance, and swimming shovelers typically draw attention to the bill by holding it angled down toward the water.

What often strikes your eye first, however, is the shoveler's dazzling and colorful plumage. Males in breeding plumage display five clearly defined patches of color—a dark green Mallardlike head, a snow-white breast, bright chestnut flanks, a white hip patch, and black under the tail. Female shovelers are mottled brown and at a glance look similar to female Blue-winged Teals, but a good look at the bill will usually answer any questions about identification. All shovelers have white wing linings and, on the upper wing adjacent to the body, large blue patches; these patches are bright light blue on males and muted blue-gray on females. A white stripe, broader on males than females, separates the patch and a dark emerald speculum.

Northern Shovelers breed throughout much of western North America. They winter principally in California, along the Gulf coast of Louisiana and Texas, and in Central America and the Caribbean.

LOOK FOR a huge, shovel-shaped bill, dark green head, white breast, and chestnut sides.

female

Garganey

Anas querquedula

male

TONY MERCIECA

Garganeys breed from Britain and France to central Europe and show up regularly in North America only on the westernmost of Alaska's remote Aleutian Islands. Vagrants have been known to show up in marshy ponds in more accessible locations on rare occasions, usually in spring and often in flocks of Blue-winged Teals.

Adult male Garganeys are smaller than Mallards and look square-headed. They are darker in the front than in the back. Look for light brown feathers near the tail, gray flanks edged in white, and a purplish

© SAM FRIED / VIREO

female

brown head and breast. A broad white stripe, the duck's most distinctive field mark, curls over each eye and down the back of the head. When male Garganeys fly, look on their underside for a white belly that contrasts sharply with a dark breast. Look also for white wing linings that contrast with the bold black front, or leading, edges of the wings. The upper sides of the male's wings are silvery.

Females are mottled brown and look very much like female Blue-winged Teals. Both species have a dark crown and a dark stripe through the eye, but the Garganey also has a white spot at the base of the bill and an additional dark stripe, or the hint of one, extending from the corner of its mouth onto its cheek.

LOOK FOR gray flanks edged in white, a purplish brown head, and a broad white stripe over the eye.

Cinnamon Teal

Anas cyanoptera

male

Cinnamon Teals breed across the western United States; they are hardly ever seen east of the Mississippi. They frequent marshes and freshwater ponds and, like other teals, rarely tip up when foraging. Instead, they swim with their bill in the water.

Male Cinnamon Teals in their breeding finery are unmistakable and beautiful. They have black under the tail and brown and tan on their back but otherwise wear essentially one color: a sleek coat of rich, warm reddish brown feathers that covers the head, neck, breast, and flanks. They view the world through scarlet eyes. Adult females are mottled brown and nearly identical to Blue-winged Teals. You can recognize female Cinnamon Teals by their warm overall tone, their face, which is plain-looking—lacking a distinct line through the eye—and their bill, which appears long and grows thicker and broader toward the tip, like the bill of a Northern Shoveler.

When Cinnamon Teals of either sex take to the air, look for markings on their upper wings that are similar to those of Blue-winged Teals: a bright blue patch adjacent to the body with a white stripe, broader on males than females, along its trailing edge.

LOOK FOR a richly colored cinnamon duck with black feathers under the tail and a blue patch on the upper wing, visible in flight.

female

Blue-winged Teal

Anas discors

male

Blue-winged Teals are handsome dabbling ducks that are noticeably smaller than Mallards. They winter in the West Indies and as far south as Chile but breed in the north-central United States and prairie Canada. They are often seen while swimming with their bill in the water.

During breeding season, adult male Blue-winged Teals are distinguished by their densely spotted cinnamon-buff sides, violet-gray head, and two distinct patches of clean, white feathers. One, a prominent crescent between the bill and eye, is the bird's most recognizable field mark, noticeable even when viewed from a distance. The other, a rounded patch on the flanks behind the leg, borders the bird's jet-black undertail feathers. Female blue-wings look different than males. Mottled brown, they have whitish feathers at the base of the bill and on the throat, a thin dark line through the eye, and white crescents above and below the eye.

Both male and female blue-wings have a large chalky blue patch on their upper wing adjacent to the body. Usually hidden from view when

female

the ducks are swimming with wings folded, the patch is obvious in flight, and diagnostic. A white stripe, broader on males than females, lines the patch's trailing edge.

LOOK FOR spotted cinnamon-buff body feathers, a violet-gray head with a white crescent, and a chalky blue patch on the upper wing.

Green-winged Teal

Anas crecca

male

The Green-winged Teal is a compact, short duck about half as long as a Mallard and less than half as heavy; it is the smallest dabbling duck in North America. It is also a fast, agile flyer, common in marshes, ponds, and flooded fields.

Adult male Green-winged Teals have a cinnamon-colored head, gray sides, and black undertail coverts—and a telling field mark to be noticed in each of three areas: On the head, look for an arching iridescent green stripe that sweeps from the eye to the back of the neck. On the sides, a short white stripe descends from in front of the folded wing to the water-line. And under the tail, look for a pair of yellowish triangular patches.

These are all reliable identifiers even when the duck is viewed from a great distance.

Female green-wings, which are mottled brown, look like female Blue-winged Teals but have steeper foreheads, a darker eyeline, and a narrow, gray bill. The patches under their tail are buff, not yellowish. And feathers along the trailing edge of the upper wings of male and female green-wings alike form a panel of shimmering green and black. A tan stripe lines the leading edge of the panel, and a white stripe marks the trailing edge.

LOOK FOR yellowish feathers under the tail, gray sides with a white vertical stripe, and a cinnamon head marked broadly with green.

TONY MERCIECA

female

Fulvous Whistling-Duck

Dendrocygna bicolor

Two species of whistling-ducks occur in North America, but you are unlikely to find either one outside of southeastern Arizona, South Texas, parts of the Gulf coast, or southern Florida. The whistling-duck's long neck and legs make it look like a cross between a goose and a duck, but its size, about that of a duck, will tell you that it's no goose. Whistling-ducks were named after their whistling calls, often given in flight.

Male Fulvous Whistling-Ducks are slightly larger than females, but otherwise the sexes are indistinguishable. Both are subtly patterned and beautiful. Look for a long-necked, essentially two-toned bird: The Fulvous Whistling-Duck's light face, chest, and belly are the color of butterscotch (the word *fulvous* means dull, brownish yellow); its dark back, wings, and tail are brownish black. Ivory tips on tawny side feathers create a whitish stripe that defines the area where the undersides meet the uppers. The duck's bill is dark gray, and its legs blue-gray.

Feathers on the back and upper wings have handsome reddish brown edges that are visible up close, but in flight the wings simply look dark, above and below. They contrast sharply with the bird's butterscotch body. Look also for bright white feathers under the tail and a crescent-shaped band of white between the dark tail and lower back.

LOOK FOR a butterscotch-colored face, chest, and body; a dark back and wings; a white band on the rump; and a gray bill and legs.

adult

Black-bellied Whistling-Duck

Dendrocygna autumnalis

Black-bellied Whistling-Ducks occur in Asia and Africa as well as North America but, like their Fulvous relatives, are not likely to be found in the Western Hemisphere away from marshes and irrigated land in coastal Mexico, the West Indies, parts of the Gulf coast, and southern Florida.

Black-bellied Whistling-Ducks perch in trees frequently, and they enjoy each other's company; you are most likely to see them in a flock, often near ponds. Individual birds are boldly partitioned into sharply defined patches of gray, rust, and black, and their nonfeathered parts are even bolder: The bill is bright red, the legs pink. Look for a pale gray face, red-brown chest, and jet-black belly and rump. When Black-bellied Whistling-Ducks spread their wings to stretch or fly, white feathers on the top of the wing form a broad white stripe that contrasts with the dark trailing edge. The undersides of their wings are dark.

Male and female Black-bellied Whistling-Ducks look alike.

LOOK FOR a gray head, rusty chest, black belly and rump, bright red bill, and pink legs.

adult

Muscovy Duck

Cairina moschata

Muscovy Ducks live in wooded lakes and marshes along both coasts of Mexico, throughout the Yucatan Peninsula, and in South America as far south as northern Argentina. They make their nests in cavities in trees but, like Wood Ducks, will also make themselves at home in boxes. Indeed, a nest-box program in northeastern Mexico is believed to have facilitated the ducks' movement northward to the region along the lower Rio Grande in South Texas. Consequently, the Falcon Dam area is now the only place where wild members of the species can be found in the United States. There are feral populations of domestic Muscovies in Florida, Texas, and other locations; these are once-domesticated birds and their offspring now living and breeding in the wild.

Wild Muscovies are wary and usually seen alone or with another Muscovy, but never in a flock, and almost always at dawn or dusk. They are bulky, gooselike birds with heavy, long tails, short legs, and pinkish bills that are mottled black. Except for a panel of white feathers on the upper wing and white wing linings, males and females are completely black. (Domestic Muscovies always have white patches somewhere on the head and body.) Watch for greenish or purplish iridescence when the sun lights them well. Males have many warty protuberances on the base of their bill and a crest on the head. Females are smaller and have fewer bumps and no crest.

LOOK FOR a bulky, black bird with a long tail, white patches on the wings, and warty protuberances on the base of the bill.

adult

TONY MERCIECA

Wood Duck

Aix sponsa

male

Wood Ducks are common in wooded swamps, rivers, and fresh-water marshes across all of North America except the Great Plains, treeless parts of the West, and Southwest. They make their nests in cavities in trees and take readily to man-made next boxes. Usually quiet, female Wood Ducks can make a loud alarm call when flushed.

Male and female woodies look dramatically different from each other. Females wear a drab coat of speckled gray-brown year-round. A white teardrop-shaped patch around the eyes is their best field mark. Males, by contrast, almost always wear the gaudy costume of a circus performer. Their shape and bold markings are distinctive even when viewed from a distance. Look for a long tail that is usually tilted up, a purple-green crest that droops from the back of the head, and gold flanks that contrast sharply with reddish violet feathers under the tail and burgundy feathers on the breast. Up close, look for bright red eyes; a white throat; white

female Wood Duck

fingerlike stripes on the chest and throat; and a red, yellow, and black bill that is lined with white.

Wood Ducks often perch in trees, and they are never seen in flocks. When they fly, their white belly contrasts with their dark breast and wings. Look for a short neck; a long, dark, rectangular tail; and a thin line of white on the trailing edge of the inner wing.

LOOK FOR golden flanks, a white throat, and a drooping crest on males; spotted gray-brown flanks and a white teardrop around the eyes on females.

2

DIVING DUCKS

Diving ducks feed on aquatic creatures and plant material by diving well below the surface of the water, sometimes to depths of more than a hundred feet. They often resurface in a different spot from where they started. Unlike dabbling ducks, diving ducks usually frequent large expanses of open water. They require a long stretch of "runway" in order to get airborne, which they do after skittering along the water's surface, beating their wings deeply. Their legs are positioned far back on their bodies—helpful for diving, but not good for walking. Many diving ducks spend their winters in the ocean or in brackish waters near the coast.

Canvasback

Aythya valisineria

male

Canvasbacks are large ducks, about the size of Mallards. They gather in winter in big flocks on deep lakes and ocean bays, often with Redheads and scaup, and they forage while diving underwater.

Adult female Canvasbacks have light brown heads and breasts, light gray backs, and dull brownish gray sides. Males wear a patchwork of monochromatic colors: black on their breast; pale gray, almost white, on their back and sides; and black above and below the tail. Their head and neck are one color as well—reddish brown.

This duck's best field mark, however, is not its plumage, but its peaked head, sloping forehead, and long, wedge-shaped bill. Males and females alike have a unique facial profile that some observers compare to a ski jump. The shape is easy to make out even at substantial distances, and it is a foolproof way to tell Canvasbacks from Redheads, which wear similar colors.

Like all diving ducks, Canvasbacks need a running start before they can lift themselves off the water. Once they are airborne, look for the male's white wing linings and the sharp contrast between the white belly and black breast.

LOOK FOR pale gray sides, black breast, reddish brown head, and long, wedge-shaped bill.

female

Redhead

Aythya americana

male

Adult male Redheads are starkly patterned diving ducks with black hindquarters and breasts, smoky gray backs and sides, and bright, shiny, reddish brown heads and necks. At first glance, they might be mistaken for Canvasbacks, which wear similar colors on the same body parts, but a closer look is sure to reveal differences in head shape, and especially in the shape and color of the bill, that will distinguish the Redheads.

A triangular bill and sloping forehead combine to make the Canvasback's head appear wedge-shaped. On the Redhead, the forehead and bill

female

meet at a sharp angle, the forehead rises high, and the head looks round. Moreover, the Redhead's bill is blue-gray, and it ends in a smart-looking black tip bounded by a thin white ring. Canvasbacks' bills are all black. The bodies of Redheads also usually look darker than Canvasbacks.

Female Redheads are brownish gray overall, and their heads are plain. Their bills, like those of males, have black tips, but the accompanying white ring is often obscure. When either male or female Redheads fly, look on the upper wings for a pale gray stripe on the trailing edge that contrasts with dark forewings.

LOOK FOR a smoky gray body, black breast, and bright reddish brown head with a black-tipped, blue-gray bill.

Tufted Duck

Aythya fuligula

TONY MERCIECA

male

Tufted Ducks do not breed in North America; they breed in Iceland and Great Britain and across Europe and Asia. In the United States, they are regular visitors only to western Alaska, usually in winter, but lucky bird-watchers occasionally spot them along the Pacific and Atlantic coasts and (rarely) on the Great Lakes, so it pays to keep an eye out for them.

Both Tufted Ducks and Ring-necked Ducks look short-bodied and large-headed. They are the same size and have similar coloring. Adult males of both species have black heads, breasts, backs, and rumps, and black-tipped, gray bills. But the bill on the Tufted Duck lacks the Ring-necked Duck's white outline, and the Tufted Duck's flanks are gleaming white, not gray like the ring-necked's. Moreover, its head is rounded in profile, not angular.

© MORTEN STRANGE/VIREO

female with chick

Female Tufted Ducks are dark brown above with blotchy brown flanks. They often have a whitish patch between the eye and bill. Both males and females sport a tuft of short feathers, or a hint of one, projecting from the back of the head. The tuft is long, drooping, and distinctive on males. In flight, both sexes show white wing linings. White feathers line the trailing edge of the Tufted Duck's dark upper wings.

LOOK FOR a black head, breast, and back; white sides; and a long, drooping crest.

Ring-necked Duck

Aythya collaris

male

One look at this small-bodied, big-headed duck, and you will wonder why it isn't called the Ring-billed rather than Ring-necked Duck. In fact, it got its name from a ring of feathers on the lower neck of the drake (the male duck). The collar is dark chestnut and often incomplete in front, so it's difficult to see, but it's there.

Much easier to spot, even from a distance, is the adult male Ring-necked Duck's black head, breast, back, and rump and its gray sides. Look for a white streak separating the breast and flanks in front of the folded wing. Notice as well the peak at the back of the ring-necked's crown and how steeply the forehead rises to it. They give the duck not only an angular profile but also an indentation between the crown and the back of the neck (the nape). Don't pass up a chance to study that distinctively marked bill. Not only does it have a black tip and a white ring, but it has a white outline as well.

Female Ring-necked Ducks are grayish brown overall, although their heads are grayer and darker than their bodies. A white ring surrounds each eye, and a short, pale white line trails behind it. In flight, gray feathers line the trailing edge of the duck's dark upper wings.

LOOK FOR a black head, breast, and back; gray sides; and a white streak between the flanks and breast.

female

Greater Scaup

Aythya marila

male

Greater Scaup (pronounced "skawp") are large diving ducks that breed in western Alaska and Arctic Canada, far to the north of the lower forty-eight states. They spend the winter in large flocks, primarily on marine waters of the Pacific and Atlantic coasts and ice-free portions of the Great Lakes. They seem to prefer large, open lakes and bays.

Because both Greater Scaup and Lesser Scaup wear essentially identical plumage, telling one from the other is a challenge, to say the least, even for experienced duck-watchers. Identifying correctly relies less on recognizing field marks than on making judgments about subtle differences, mostly in size and shape.

Adult females of both species are brown with white patches at the base of the bill, but Greater Scaup often have an additional mark, a pale white crescent on their cheeks. Males of both species are glossy black in front and at the tail end and whitish in the middle. But the male Greater Scaup appears large and bulky, its flanks look clean white, and, especially when the bird is relaxed, its head and neck appear thick, almost bulbous. What's more, if the sunlight strikes the bird just so, you might be able to detect a greenish iridescence on the Greater Scaup's head.

The scaup's name is derived from its favorite food source; shellfish are found in beds once known as scalps or scaups.

LOOK FOR clean white flanks; a thick head and neck; and, in good light, greenish iridescence on the head.

female

Lesser Scaup

Aythya affinis

male

Lesser Scaup are smaller than Greater Scaup. They breed from central Alaska to Quebec and locally in the West, and they spend the winter primarily on freshwater bays and wetlands across the United States and on fresh to brackish water along the southern Atlantic coast and the Gulf and Pacific coasts. Like Greater Scaup, they form large flocks during fall and winter but seem to prefer sheltered bays, inlets, and lakes more than open water.

female

The lesser's plumage is nearly identical to that of the Greater Scaup. Distinguishing the two species in the field is difficult and depends less on recognizing field marks than it does on judging subtle differences in size and shape.

Females of both species of scaup are brown with white patches at the base of the bill. Both males are black in front and at the tail end and whitish in the middle. And both sexes of both species have blue-gray bills, the reason for the birds' descriptive nickname—the Bluebill. But the Lesser Scaup's head looks taller and narrower, its bill looks thinner and straighter, and, especially when the bird is relaxed, the peak of its head forms a "corner" at the rear of the crown. Look for purple iridescence on the head.

LOOK FOR a tall, narrow head; a thin, straight bill; and a corner at the rear of the crown.

Common Eider

Somateria mollissima

male

Common Eiders are the largest ducks in the Northern Hemisphere. They breed at the northern edge of the continent and can be found year-round along the coasts of southwestern Alaska, Newfoundland, the Gulf of Saint Lawrence, and from Nova Scotia to Cape Cod. In winter, they range farther along the southern coast of Alaska and as far south as coastal Virginia.

Breeding males look largely black when viewed from behind and largely white from the front. Their face, breast, and back are white; their flanks and rear end are black; and they have white thigh patches and distinctive black crowns. Female Common Eiders are plainer, generally brown, but vary across the continent from silvery gray to dark reddish brown. Barred feathers on the flanks and back give the females a striped look that helps tell them from King Eiders. The species' best field mark, however, is its shape: Males and females alike have short necks, large heads, and long, wedge-shaped bills. A triangular patch of feathers, white on males and grayish or brown on females, reaches from the cheeks to the nostrils.

Common Eiders fly low in lines. In flight, they appear heavy and gooselike. Look on males for black primary and secondary feathers (the longest on the wings) that contrast sharply with the all-white back and upper wings.

Eiderdown, the bird's soft insulating feathers, is used to fill high-priced comforters, quilts, and coats. The material is hand-gathered from eider nests, where the bird placed it to keep hatchlings warm.

LOOK FOR black sides, white breast, large black-crowned head, and long, wedge-shaped bill.

female

King Eider

Somateria spectabilis

Hardy King Eiders breed in the Arctic, near the top of the world. Few birds breed farther north. They migrate in huge flocks and spend the winter along the Aleutian Islands and the southern coast of mainland Alaska and, on the eastern side of the continent, along Labrador and Newfoundland, in the Gulf of Saint Lawrence, and (in small numbers) along the Atlantic coast as far south as Virginia.

Adult male King Eiders in breeding plumage are spectacular. Their flanks, lower back, and rear end are black, but their upper back is white, their breast is white washed with salmon-pink, and their head is light blue-gray. White patches stand out near the rump, and a large yellow-orange knob sits atop their red bill, dominating the front of the face and making the head look blocklike. When King Eiders fly, watch for white patches on otherwise all-black upper wings.

Females have a conventional dark bill and are reddish brown over-all. A thin pale line runs through their eyes and curls downward behind them. Look closely at the female's body feathers: Black chevron-shaped marks on each one combine to make the flanks and back look scalloped. Similar feathers on female Common Eiders are barred, giving the birds a striped look.

LOOK FOR black sides, a light breast, and a blue-gray head with a large yellow-orange knob above the bill.

TONY MERCIECA

male (in back) and female

Spectacled Eider

Somateria fischeri

male
TONY MERCIECA

It's a shame that such a handsome bird lives in regions so remote. Spectacled Eiders breed in western Alaska only in the Yukon-Kuskokwim Delta and along the Beaufort and Chukchi Seas and in coastal wetlands in Arctic Russia. The ducks migrate after breeding but don't travel far; they spend the winter primarily in the Bering Sea south of Saint Lawrence Island, swimming in open leads and holes in the pack ice. This increasingly rare species is listed as threatened throughout its range.

Spectacled Eiders are medium-size sea ducks, larger than Steller's Eiders but smaller than Common Eiders. Adult males have a blackish gray breast, sides, and rump and a white throat, upper neck, and back. Their head is dome-shaped and boldly marked with large, rounded patches of silvery white feathers around each eye (their spectacles). Gray-green feathers on the nape and the region between the eyes and the bill give the face a dirty appearance and make the patches conspicuous. Spectacles, albeit duller ones, are also apparent on females, which are pale brown overall. Barring on their body feathers creates a striped appearance, similar to that of Common Eiders.

Spectacled Eiders often fly in lines. When males are in flight, look for their blackish breast, which distinguishes them from all other eiders.

LOOK FOR blackish gray breast, sides, and rump; a white back; and a round silvery white patch around each eye.

TONY MERCIECA

female

Steller's Eider

Polysticta stelleri

male   TONY MERCIECA

To see Steller's Eiders, you have to go to Alaska. They breed along its remote north coast, and they spend the winter in the eastern Aleutian Islands and along the southern side of the Alaska Peninsula. Like Spectacled Eiders, the other Alaska-only eider species, few individual Steller's Eiders venture south of Alaskan waters.

Steller's Eiders are the smallest and lightest of the four eider species. They weigh less than half as much as King Eiders. They have a flat crown

TONY MERCIECA

female

and a steep forehead and nape, an unremarkable gray bill, and long, narrow wings that enable them to lift easily from the water. Adult males appear mostly white, especially when viewed from a distance, but are dramatically marked with bluish black on the throat, neck, back, and rump. Their breast is washed with peach. Look for a dark smudge between the eye and bill and three characteristic dark spots: one around the eye, another on the back of the head, and a third on the side of the breast in front of the wing. When males fly, the upper surface of their wings is extensively white.

Female Steller's Eiders are dark brown. When they lift their wings to stretch or fly, look for a blue speculum bordered, Mallardlike, by bold white bars on its leading and trailing edges.

LOOK FOR a peach breast; bluish black throat and neck; and white head with a smudge in front of the eye, a dark spot around it, and a dark patch on the nape.

Harlequin Duck

Histrionicus histrionicus

male

Rugged Harlequin Ducks thrive in rushing, churning water. They breed in the northeastern and northwestern corners of the continent and spend the winter along the rocky coastlines of southern Alaska and British Columbia in the West and Nova Scotia and New England in the East. Each winter, more than half the eastern population of Harlequins can be found along the coast of Maine.

Adult males wear Brooks Brothers blue overall with black rumps and warm chestnut-colored sides. White stripes make their plumage dazzling: One, a horizontal bar formed by feathers on the back, runs almost the length of the body above the flanks. Another rises up from the breast to the wing. A third stripe encircles the neck. And a fourth, a thin vertical

female

streak, marks the back of the head. As if that weren't enough, a bright white crescent fills the region between the eyes and bill. Behind each eye is a white dot.

Female Harlequins are brown overall. Look for a stubby gray bill, steep forehead, and three white patches on the face: a bright circular or oval patch behind the eye, a muted triangle between the eyes and bill, and a small mark above and in front of the eye.

LOOK FOR a slate blue duck with chestnut sides, two white bars on the breast, and a white crescent on the face.

Long-tailed Duck

Clangula hyemalis

Long-tailed Ducks were named for the pair of elongated black central tail feathers that stream behind the birds as they fly, but only adult males possess them. (A better name might have been short-necked duck, for that is a feature shared by both sexes.) They were once known as Old-squaw. The species breeds across northernmost North America, then moves south to spend the winter off the Atlantic and Pacific coasts and on the Great Lakes and the Saint Lawrence.

Male and female long-tails do not look alike, and both sexes wear generally darker plumage on their breeding grounds than they do in fall and winter, when you are most likely to see them. Males in their winter plumage are handsome and eye-catching. White feathers under the tail

male in spring plumage

male in winter plumage

TONY MERCIECA

female in winter plumage

and on the upper breast and neck contrast sharply with dark wings. The head is boldly marked: The crown is white, a gray area surrounds each eye, and black patches adorn the cheeks and sides of the neck. The bill is dark blue-gray and has a pink band.

Nonbreeding females have squarish heads and appear pale, less contrasty. They have white flanks, brown breasts, and white faces with dark brown crowns. Their best field mark is a large dark brown patch on the lower cheek.

LOOK FOR elongated central tail feathers, dark wings, and a white and gray head with a black patch on the lower cheek.

Surf Scoter

Melanitta perspicillata

male

The scoters (pronounced with a long *o*) can be found along the coasts of North America during winter. Each is essentially all black, so telling the different species apart can present a challenge, especially when the ducks are viewed from a distance. To identify them, study the shape and color of the bill, look for markings on the head and wings, and pay attention to the way the ducks dive.

Surf Scoters are unique because they breed in North America only. (The other two scoters also breed in Eurasia.) In winter they can be found as far south as Baja California and Florida. Their heads are square-shaped, and they have large, thick bills. As a result, Surf Scoters tend to look head-heavy, their profile flat. Lustrous black adult males have two well-defined white patches on their head—one on the forehead just above the bill, the other on the back of their head. Their bill is multicolored: red, orange, and white, with yellow at the tip and a large black dot on either side.

Female Surf Scoters are dark brown and have less-conspicuous green-black bills. Look for three indistinct pale white patches on their heads: between their eye and bill, behind the eye, and on the back of the head. In flight, Surf Scoters' wings are uniformly dark, top and bottom. When they dive, they leap and flick their wings.

LOOK FOR an all-black duck with white patches on the forehead and nape and a thick orange, white, and black bill.

female

Black Scoter

Melanitta nigra

female

Glossy black from forehead to tail, adult male Black Scoters have one obvious field mark: their uniform blackness. No white patches mark their forehead or nape, as on Surf Scoters, and there are no white panels on the trailing edges of their wings, as on White-winged Scoters. Even their eyes are dark. But their blackness isn't the Black Scoter's only distinguishing feature. Their bills sport large yellow-orange knobs that contrast sharply with their all-black faces and are easy to see, even from a distance.

Females can be recognized by their two-toned heads and ordinary-looking bills. Their cheeks are pale and grayish, while their crown and nape are dark and sooty. The cap and cheeks meet in a sharply drawn line that passes just below the eyes and runs down the sides of the neck. The female's bill lacks the yellow knob of the male and is not as conspicuous; it is thinner than the bills of either Surf Scoters or White-winged Scoters.

When Black Scoters fly, look on the wings for silvery primary feathers and coverts. They contrast with the black feathers closer to the duck's body. And watch how Black Scoters dive: They leap and hold their wings tight against their body.

LOOK FOR an all-black duck with a yellow-orange knob on its bill and two-toned underwings.

male

White-winged Scoter

Melanitta fusca

male

White-winged Scoters, the largest of the three scoter species, are stocky birds with thick-looking necks and wedge-shaped bills. They do not leap when they dive.

Like male Surf Scoters, adult male White-winged Scoters are velvety black all over. A black knob grows atop the bill, and a comma-shaped white mark often appears behind and below the eye, but it can be difficult to see. More reliable as a field mark is the white wing patch for which the scoter was named. Formed by all-white feathers on the trailing edge of the wing, the patch is obvious on birds in flight but is often covered up on

female

swimming birds. You may not be able to spot it at first glance, but if you are patient, the duck might rearrange its wings enough for either a thin white line or a small white square to peek out above the flanks just forward of the rump.

The patch is also useful for identifying female White-winged Scoters, which are sooty brown overall and have dark gray bills. Most have large, diffuse, pale patches between their eyes and bill and smaller, distinct patches behind their eyes. Look carefully at females' profile: The ridge running from the forehead to the tip of the bill is slightly concave. On Surf Scoters, it is always either straight or convex.

LOOK FOR an all-black duck with white panels on the trailing edges of its wings.

Common Goldeneye

Bucephala clangula

male

Common Goldeneyes breed in northern forests worldwide—in North America, from Alaska to Newfoundland. In winter, they can be found in shallow bays and harbors along the Atlantic and Pacific coasts and on large lakes and rivers across the interior United States.

Adult male Common Goldeneyes are stunning. They have black backs and tail ends, pure white flanks and breasts, and iridescent green-black heads. Their bills are blue-black, and on each side of the face a white oval spot marks the area below and in front of the eye. Female Common Goldeneyes are less starkly patterned: They have gray backs and sides

male and female (in front)

and chocolate brown heads. Their bills are dabbed with yellow, either at the tip or in a band across the middle.

On the Pacific coast, in the Gulf of Saint Lawrence, and in New England, you may find Common Goldeneyes associating with similar-looking Barrow's Goldeneyes. To tell the species apart, look closely at the faces. Barrow's are marked with a white crescent, not a white oval. Then examine the shape and size of the heads and bills. Common Goldeneyes have bigger bills, sloping foreheads, and more peaked heads. Both species have white patches on the trailing edges of their wings, adjacent to the body, but the patches are wider on Common Goldeneyes.

LOOK FOR a black back, white flanks and breast, and a green-black head with a white oval below and in front of the eye.

Barrow's Goldeneye

Bucephala islandica

male   TONY MERCIECA

Ninety percent of the world population of Barrow's Goldeneyes breeds west of the Rockies from Alaska to California. (The remainder nest in Iceland and along the north shore of the Saint Lawrence River in Quebec.) In winter they can be found in coastal waters from Kodiak Island, Alaska, to Puget Sound as well as on rivers and lakes in the West as far south as northern New Mexico, and in the Gulf of Saint Lawrence, the Canadian Maritimes, and coastal New England.

Adult male Barrow's Goldeneyes have purple-black heads, white flanks and breasts, and black backs and rear ends. They look blacker than Common Goldeneyes and have a conspicuous mark that commons lack: a vertical black bar between their flanks and breast. Barrow's bills are blue-black, and on each side of the face, a white crescent (not an oval) marks the area between the eye and bill. Females have gray backs and sides and dark brown heads. Their bills are usually mostly yellow.

On the Pacific coast and in the Northeast, you may find Barrow's Goldeneyes associating with Common Goldeneyes. To tell the species apart, look closely at the shape and size of the ducks' heads and bills. Barrow's Goldeneyes have short, stubby bills and bushy, oblong napes, and their foreheads rise steeply, almost vertically, from the base of the bill.

LOOK FOR a black back, white flanks and breast, and a purple-black head with a white crescent in front of the eye.

TONY MERCIECA

female

Bufflehead

Bucephala albeola

male

Buffleheads are members of the same family as Common and Barrow's Goldeneyes and, like them, they nest in tree cavities. But they are much smaller, compact and toylike, weighing only about half as much as their siblings. Buffleheads bob up and down on the water when they surface after diving. Look for them in winter in small flocks on lakes and bays and along the Pacific coast from British Columbia to California and the Atlantic coast from New Jersey to South Carolina.

Adult male Buffleheads are every bit as striking as adult Goldeneyes. Their backs and necks are black, and their flanks and breasts are gleaming white—so white that they might catch your eye even when the ducks are swimming at a distance. Their best field mark, however, is on their head, just behind the eyes: broad white patches that grow wider toward the back of the head and meet at the nape. These marks are usually easy to spot from a distance, and they're unmistakable; only Hooded Mergansers have anything like them.

Female Buffleheads are less contrasty than males. Their heads, backs, and wings are dark brown; their sides are pale gray, not white. They too have a distinctive field mark: a white oval ear patch located below and behind each eye.

LOOK FOR a white breast and sides, a black back, and a black and white head.

female

Hooded Merganser

Lophodytes cucullatus

male

The Hooded Merganser is the smallest of the three mergansers that live in North America—it weighs two pounds less than a Common Merganser and is half a foot shorter—and it is the only merganser native to the continent. It breeds in forested wetlands, swamps, and beaver ponds throughout the eastern United States and in the Pacific Northwest and southern Canada. It can be found year-round, usually alone or in pairs, rarely in a group, throughout most of its range. Like all mergansers, Hooded Mergansers have long, thin bills with serrated edges that help them catch slippery fish.

Richly colored and boldly patterned, adult male hoodeds will make you happy you own binoculars—or wish you did. Their flanks are chestnut brown; their backs, necks, heads, and bills are black; and pairs of

female

jaunty black stripes border the white breast. The ducks' best field mark, however, is their extraordinary crest. Sailcloth white and edged in black, it is sure to catch your eye even from a distance. It can be raised and lowered like a spinnaker on a low-slung yacht, exposing either a wide snowy patch or a thick horizontal streak behind each eye.

Female Hooded Mergansers are drabber than the males. Their plumage is grayish brown overall. Their bill is a mundane blackish green with orange edges. (Both Common and Red-breasted Mergansers have orange-red bills.) What distinguishes the females is their bushy brown crests, which are tipped with cinnamon. In the right light, the crests glow.

LOOK FOR a black back, chestnut sides, white breast, and black head with a white crest.

Common Merganser

Mergus merganser

male   TONY MERCIECA

Common Mergansers breed in northern North America and in the western and northeastern United States. After breeding, they congregate in large single-species flocks along both coasts and on lakes, rivers, and reservoirs in every state except those in the northern Great Plains and Southeast. They seem to prefer fresh water.

Common Mergansers are long-bodied, tapered diving ducks whose colorful markings do not blend but meet in clean lines. Adult males have black backs and gray tails that contrast with their gleaming white sides and breasts. Their heads look black when viewed from a distance and reflect iridescent green highlights close up. Females have gray tails, backs, and sides; whitish upper breasts; and rusty brown heads. Look on the neck for a crisp lower boundary to the brown feathers and a clearly defined small patch of white under the base of the bill. These marks will help you tell female Common from female Red-breasted Mergansers.

Both male and female Common Mergansers have swept-back crests, but the crests are conspicuous only on females. More diagnostic are the mergansers' long, sloping foreheads and bright scarlet-orange bills. The bills are deep at the base and narrow toward the tip and end with a small but noticeable hook.

Both Common Mergansers and Red-breasted Mergansers have white patches on their upper, inner wings. Look for a sharp line of contrast between the dark head and white breast of the male Common Merganser.

LOOK FOR a gleaming white breast and sides, greenish black head, and tapered orange-red bill.

female

Red-breasted Merganser

Mergus serrator

male

Red-breasted Mergansers breed in northern and tundra environments across North America from Alaska in the west to Baffin Island, Labrador, and Newfoundland in the east. Some spend the winter on the Great Lakes and the Great Salt Lake and along the Pacific coast from Alaska to Baja California. Others winter along the Atlantic and Gulf coasts as far south as northern Mexico. They seem to prefer saltwater.

Unlike male Common Mergansers, which look white when seen from a distance, adult male Red-breasted Mergansers appear dark. Their sides and flanks are gray, their backs are black, and their breasts are reddish brown, dotted with black speckles. Their heads are greenish black, like Common Mergansers, but red-breasteds have shaggy, double-pointed crests, and their eyes are red. Common Mergansers have manelike crests and dark brown eyes.

Female Red-breasted Mergansers have grayish brown bodies; whitish chins, throats, and breasts; and olive-brown heads and crests. They are easy to confuse with female Common Mergansers. To tell them apart, study the areas where different colors meet. No boundaries on red-breasteds are sharply drawn lines, as on the common; rather, the colors blend into each other. Moreover, the bills of Common Mergansers are wedge-shaped. On red-breasteds, they are thin from base to tip, and they curve up slightly along their length.

LOOK FOR gray sides, reddish brown breast, and greenish black head with a double-pointed crest, and thin orange-red bill.

female

Masked Duck

Nomonyx dominicus

male

The Masked Duck is a tropical species that lurks in vegetation-covered ponds and lakes in Mexico and the West Indies, in Central America, and as far south as northwest Peru and central Argentina. In the United States, it has been known to visit Louisiana and Florida, but only irregularly, and it resides only in Texas, where breeding was confirmed for the first time in 1967.

Masked Ducks are stiff-tails. The feathers of their tails are elongated and rigid. The birds use them as rudders when swimming underwater and often, but not always, hold them upright while paddling on the surface. Unlike most diving ducks, they do not need to run in order to take off; after diving, they often appear to leave the water flying. Look on their wings near the body for a comma-shaped white patch.

female

It is the adult male Masked Duck that wears the mask. Males are a rich reddish brown overall, with back and wing feathers dabbed with black. Their napes are reddish brown. Their foreheads, throats, and cheeks (their mask) are glossy black. A thin, light blue ring surrounds each eye, and their bill is blue with a black tip. Females lack the males' warm-hued coloration. Their heads look zebralike because dark brown horizontal stripes—on the crown, through each eye, and running from the bill across the cheeks—contrast sharply with their buff-colored eyebrows and cheeks.

LOOK FOR a reddish brown breast, neck, and nape; black on the sides and crown; and a stiff tail.

male Ruddy Duck

Ruddy Duck

Oxyura jamaicensis

Nesting Ruddy Ducks can be found around the Great Lakes and in South Texas, Mexico, and as far south as central El Salvador, but they breed primarily in prairie potholes in the western half of North America. After breeding, they vacate the northernmost parts, abandoning Canada completely for the time being, and fly east as well as south, spreading out across the United States. Look for them on open ponds, bays, wetlands, and impoundments, often in large flocks that include American Coots, Ring-necked Ducks, and Buffleheads.

female

Ruddies are small, stocky ducks with big heads, sizable bills, and stiff tails that the birds often hold upright, especially when they are dozing. They run across the water before they take off. Breeding males wear three colors in three discrete patches: Their necks, breasts, and bodies are bright reddish brown. Their cheeks are bright white. And the top and back of their heads are black. The bill is sky-blue and has a black tip. The plumage worn by adult females follows the same three-patch pattern but is duller. Females' bodies are gray-brown; the patches on their cheeks are buff-gray, not white; and the head cap is blackish brown. Look for a dark horizontal stripe that runs from the corner of the mouth across their cheeks. Their bill is dark gray.

LOOK FOR a reddish brown body, white cheeks, black crown and nape, and sky-blue bill.

3

LOONS, GREBES, AND OTHER WATERBIRDS

Beginning birders sometimes confuse loons and grebes with ducks, but all three belong to different taxonomic orders. Loons, which resemble large ducks, are masterful divers; their legs are set far back on their bodies, helping them dive deeply and swiftly. But they have trouble taking even a few steps on dry land. Grebes look like small ducks and spend just about all of their lives in the water. They dive for their food, but not as deeply as most diving ducks or loons. Unlike ducks, grebes have thin, pointy bills.

A few other unrelated waterbirds—cormorants, gallinules, moorhens, and coots—often exhibit duck-like behaviors and might be mistaken for ducks at first glance.

Red-throated Loon

Gavia stellata

Red-throated Loons make their nests around the top of the world and, in North America, from Alaska east to Labrador and Newfoundland and north to Ellesmere Island. After breeding, they move south, gathering in the West along the Aleutians and Kodiak Island and as far south as coastal Baja California. In the East, they gather along the Atlantic coast from Newfoundland to Georgia. They are about the size of Pacific Loons; Common and Yellow-billed Loons are much larger.

Red-throated Loons wear bolder plumage when they are breeding than they do in fall and winter, when you are most likely to see them. Breeding adults have silky pearl-gray heads and necks, brown-black wings and backs, and white undersides. Their bills are entirely black. They sport unique patches of rust-red feathers on their throats. Nonbreeding loons lack both the throat patches and gray head feathers; their heads and necks are edged with black but mostly white. Their backs are speckled.

On the head and neck, look for a sharp boundary between the black and white feathers, and notice that the line is closer to the back of the neck than the front. The area covered by white feathers is greater on Red-throated Loons than on any other nonbreeding loon. White feathers even surround each eye. Overall shape is a good field mark, too. Red-throated Loons have tapered heads (other loons' foreheads are steeper), and their bills are narrow and straight. The birds tend to hold their bills tilted up. Plus, their heads droop when they fly, which makes the loons look hump-backed.

Like all loons, red-throateds make a variety of drawn-out wails and tremulous cries during the summer nesting season.

LOOK FOR a tapered profile, a bill held tilted up, and on nonbreeding ducks more white than black on the sides of the neck and white around each eye.

adult

Pacific Loon

Gavia pacifica

adult

Pacific Loons breed in the western and central parts of the continent's northern tier, from Alaska east to the shores of Hudson Bay and Baffin Island. They spend the winter along the Pacific coast from southeastern Alaska to Baja California and in the waters at the northern end of the Gulf of California. They are about the size of Red-throated Loons. Common and Yellow-billed Loons are much larger.

Pacific Loons wear bolder plumage when they are breeding than they do in fall and winter, when you are most likely to see them. Breeding adults have exquisite two-toned heads. Silvery gray feathers cover their napes and blend seamlessly into jet-black feathers on the face and throat. Five thin white stripes run from the shoulders up each side of the neck, and bold white spots mark the backs. The birds have black bills and reddish eyes.

Nonbreeding loons lack the neck stripes and back spots and are brownish gray above, white below. Their bills are black and gray. Dark feathers cover the top of their heads and the rear part of their necks and extend down to or slightly below each eye. Look for a crisp, dark border on each side of the neck and, occasionally, a narrow strip of dark feathers under the chin. Watch also for how swimming loons hold their heads; Pacific Loons usually hold their bills horizontal, not tilted up.

LOOK FOR dark feathers extending down to or slightly below each eye and a crisp boundary between black and white on each side of the neck on nonbreeding birds.

Common Loon

Gavia immer

adult

Common Loons nest in boreal and mixed forests across North America. Their breeding range includes parts of the Pacific Northwest, upper Midwest, and New England. The birds winter along the Pacific coast from the Aleutians south to Colima, Mexico, and along the Atlantic coast from Newfoundland south to central Florida. They are large birds, almost the size of Yellow-billed Loons. Red-throated and Pacific Loons are much smaller.

Like all loons, Common Loons wear bolder plumage when they are breeding than they do in fall and winter. Breeding adults are unmistakable. They have all-black heads and black necks. A patch of bright white stripes that is thicker in back than in front marks each side of the lower neck. White rectangles give the back and upper wings a stark, checkered look. Common Loons' bills are entirely black, their eyes red. Nonbreeding loons have fewer high-contrast lines and crisscrosses; they are gray-brown above, white below, and their bills are light gray, not black. The bill's top edge is dark, as is its tip. Common Loons tend to hold their bills horizontal.

On nonbreeding Common Loons, look for a conspicuous pale ring around each eye, a blackish half-collar wrapping around the rear of the lower neck, and just above it, a wedge of whitish feathers jutting back from the white foreneck. Head shape is always a good field mark: Common Loons have steep foreheads. At times, their crown can look concave.

LOOK FOR a bill held horizontal, steep forehead, blackish half-collar on the lower neck, and above it, a whitish wedge on nonbreeding birds.

Yellow-billed Loon

Gavia adamsii

Yellow-billed Loons nest in Alaska on the Seward Peninsula and north of the Brooks Range and in northern Canada from Great Bear and Great Slave Lakes in the Northwest Territories north and east to the Melville Peninsula. The birds winter along the Pacific coast from Kodiak Island south to Vancouver Island. They are North America's largest loon. Males can weigh almost thirteen pounds, more even than Common Loons.

Like all loons, Yellow-bills wear bolder plumage when they are breeding than they do in fall and winter. Breeding adults look similar to Common Loons. They have all-black heads and black necks and a patch of coarse, vertical, white stripes on each side of the lower neck. White rectangles, fewer and larger than on Common Loons, create a checkered pattern on the back and upper wings. Their bills are conspicuous and unique, however—yellow or ivory-colored (the bills of all other breeding loons are black), long, and oddly shaped. The top edge is straight, but the lower mandible appears beveled; its bottom edge angles up toward the tip. What's more, Yellow-billed Loons tend to hold their bills tilted up, not horizontal, as Common Loons do.

The bills are paler but still important field marks on nonbreeding Yellow-billed Loons, which otherwise look like Common Loons. They are gray-brown above and white below. Look for a steep forehead and a flat, sometimes concave, crown.

LOOK FOR an up-tilted, ivory-colored bill with a straight top edge and an angled bottom edge on nonbreeding birds.

adult

© GERRIT VYN/VIREO

Red-necked Grebe

Podiceps grisegena

adult

Red-necked, Horned, and Eared Grebes are members of the same family, but Red-necked Grebes are larger, and they alone have dark brown eyes. The other grebes have red eyes. Red-neckeds' thin, pointy bills are mostly yellow, and the distance from the corner of the mouth (the gape) to the bill's tip looks about the same as from the back of their head to the front. The other grebes' bills are proportionally smaller and black.

A swimming Red-necked Grebe in breeding plumage looks tricolored when seen from the front. A black band runs from its bill over the top of the head and down the back of the neck. A broad white patch rises from the throat, covering the area between each eye and the back of the head. And beneath the white patch, lustrous brick-red feathers bedeck the front of the neck and breast. Nonbreeding grebes look dingy in comparison. They still have the black cap but lack the red, and all that remains of the cheek patch are whitish throat and chin feathers. Look for a small patch of gray feathers behind each eye and a white extension of the chin feathers that curls upward near the rear of the face.

Red-necked Grebes breed sporadically from Alaska south to Washington, Idaho, and Montana and east to Minnesota, Wisconsin, and southwest Quebec. They spend the winter on the Great Lakes but primarily along both coasts—in the West mostly between southern Alaska and Oregon and in the East mainly from Newfoundland to Long Island, New York.

LOOK FOR a big yellow bill, black crown, broad white cheek patch, and brick-red neck and breast.

Horned Grebe

Podiceps auritus

Horned Grebes nest on lakes and ponds in northwestern North America, primarily north of the United States. Their breeding range stretches south of the Brooks Range in Alaska, east of the coast range in British Columbia, and east to Manitoba's Hudson Bay shores. Horned Grebes spend the winter on inland lakes and rivers in the southeast but loiter mostly along the coasts, in the West from the Aleutian Islands to Baja California and in the East from Nova Scotia to the Gulf.

Male and female Horned Grebes look alike. Both sexes wear more colorful plumage during nesting season than they do in autumn and winter. Breeding adults are unmistakable. They have black heads; chestnut necks, breasts, and sides; bright red eyes; and black bills. Their most stunning field mark is their "horns": conspicuous arching patches of erectable yellow-buff feathers behind each eye.

Nonbreeding birds lack horns and are similar in appearance to Eared Grebes, mostly blackish above and white below. To identify them, study the shape of their head and the boundary between the black and white feathers on their faces. Horned Grebe heads look flat on top. The highest point is toward the back of the crown, not the front. And the bird's white cheeks meet its beretlike black cap in a crisp line behind the eyes. Look also for a distinctive white spot in the region between each eye and the bill.

LOOK FOR a crisp boundary between a black crown and white cheeks and a white spot between the eye and bill on nonbreeding birds.

adult

Eared Grebe

Podiceps nigricollis

Eared Grebes breed on shallow lakes and ponds throughout the western United States and southern Canada, from British Columbia east to southwestern Manitoba and south to northern Arizona and New Mexico. In winter they gather in the tens of thousands on California's Salton Sea, but the vast majority—hundreds of thousands of birds—assembles in the Gulf of California of Mexico.

Male and female Eared Grebes look alike. Both sexes wear more colorful plumage during nesting season than they do in autumn and winter. Breeding adults have black heads, necks, and breasts (they are known in Europe as Black-necked Grebes) as well as rich cinnamon-brown sides and red eyes. Wispy golden ear tufts fan out across the sides of the head behind the eyes.

Nonbreeding birds lack the plumes and are similar in appearance to Horned Grebes, mostly blackish above and white below. To identify them, study the shape of their head and the boundary between the black and white feathers on their faces. Eared Grebe heads look round. Their foreheads are steep, forming a high peak in the front of the crown, not the rear. And black feathers are not restricted to the bird's crown. Rather, they darken the area behind and below the eyes, where they blend with the white feathers of the throat. Look also for the distinctive shape of the Eared Grebe's bill. The upper mandible is straight, but the lower mandible angles up toward the tip.

LOOK FOR a round head, steep forehead, and up-tilted bill on nonbreeding birds.

adult

TONY MERCIECA

Pied-billed Grebe

Podilymbus podiceps

adult

The Pied-billed Grebe is the only North American grebe with a short, thick, whitish bill. Our six other grebes have slender bills that are either short and black or long and yellow. Look for a conspicuous black band on the bills of Pied-billed Grebes during breeding season.

The birds can be found swimming and diving for food in freshwater marshes and lakes over much of the continent: in southern Canada from Alberta east to Nova Scotia, across the United States, and south into Mexico and Central America. Since they migrate only at night and prefer to elude predators by swimming, either by paddling behind cover or submerging, you will hardly ever see one in flight.

Pied-billed Grebes are larger than Least Grebes and are comparable in size to Horned and Eared Grebes and American Coots. They are dark brown overall, but feathers under their tails are bright white, cottony, and conspicuous, noticeable even on birds that are so far away their bills are hard to see. On grebes in breeding plumage, look for a narrow ring of bluish white feathers around each eye and black feathers on the throat, chin, and forehead. Like the band on the bill, the dark feathers will fade after breeding season.

LOOK FOR a brown body with white under the tail and a thick, whitish bill with a black band.

Least Grebe

Tachybaptus dominicus

adult

The Least Grebe is a tiny, dark bird—its average body mass, between four and six ounces, is only a quarter that of the Pied-billed Grebe. Puffy feathers around the adult's tail and on its lower back are white, but the remainder of its plumage is essentially one color throughout the year: sooty gray. Even its slender, pointed bill is dark. Its eyes are the most colorful body part; they are bright yellow.

Black feathers on the throat, forehead, crown, and nape frame the face and neck of Least Grebes in breeding plumage. At other times of the year, look for a neutral, gray-colored bill and a patch of pale feathers on the throat.

Least Grebes live across a broad expanse of the Western Hemisphere, but only in the southernmost part of North America. They breed as far south as northern Argentina, throughout the Virgin Islands, the Bahamas, the Greater Antilles, and Central America, and from the Mexico-Guatemala border north to Baja California, Sonora, and southern Texas. The area south of San Antonio is the only location where you can find them in the United States. Look for them diving or sitting motionless in quiet freshwater and brackish ponds, sloughs, and ditches.

LOOK FOR a dark gray bird with puffy white bloomers and yellow eyes.

Western Grebe

Aechmophorus occidentalis

Western Grebes breed on freshwater lakes and marshes from south-eastern British Columbia east to southern Manitoba in Canada and across the western United States. They spend the winter primarily along the Pacific coast.

Less common Clark's Grebes occur in the same general area of the continent and look almost identical. In fact, they and Western Grebes were considered the same species until 1985. Each has a slim body; a long, swanlike neck; bright red eyes; and a narrow, pointed bill. Gray or gray-ish black feathers cover the top of the head, run down the back of the neck, and spill over the back. On both species, white feathers fill the breast, the front of the neck, and part of the face.

Telling one grebe from the other during breeding season (between April and July) can be challenging, even for experienced grebe-watchers, and nearly impossible outside of breeding season (October to February), when face patterns become less distinct.

Look carefully at each bird's flanks and back, at the boundaries of the black and white feathering on its face, and especially at its bill. Western Grebes look uniformly dark on the back and sides. The upper edge of the white feathers on each side of the face falls below the eye, not above it. Feathers ranging in color from black to medium gray surround each eye. The most reliable field mark, however, and especially during winter, is bill color. On Western Grebes, it is always greenish yellow. On Clark's Grebes, it is bright orange-yellow.

LOOK FOR a greenish yellow bill and a black cap that in breeding season extends down below the eye.

adult

Clark's Grebe

Aechmophorus clarkii

adult

Clark's Grebes breed in the same part of the continent but not as far north as Western Grebes. The two were once considered the same species and look almost identical. Each has a slim body, swanlike neck, red eyes, and narrow, pointed bill. Both have white feathers on the breast, the front of the neck, and the lower part of the face, and gray or grayish black feathers on the top of the head, back of the neck, and back.

Telling the grebes apart between April and July, when they breed, can be difficult, and it is nearly impossible outside of breeding season (October to February), when face patterns become less distinct. Look carefully at each bird's flanks and back, at the boundaries of the black and white feathering on its face, and especially at its bill.

The sides of Clark's Grebes are usually speckled with white; Western Grebes are uniformly dark. The upper edges of the white feathers on Clark's Grebes' faces rises above the eyes. The areas immediately behind and above each eye may be gray, but the lores, the region between the eyes and the bill, are always white.

The most reliable field mark, especially during winter, is bill color. It is always bright orange-yellow on Clark's Grebes, and visible even from a distance. On Western Grebes, the bill is greenish yellow and less conspicuous.

LOOK FOR a bright orange-yellow bill and, in breeding season, white feathers behind, above, and in front of the eye

Double-crested Cormorant

Phalacrocorax auritus

Cormorants are large, slender birds with webbed feet and long, narrow, hooked bills. They are accomplished divers and underwater swimmers and prodigious consumers of fish.

The Double-crested Cormorant is one of six North American cormorant species, but it is the only one that appears inland as well as along the coasts. It nests in the interior of the continent and along the Saint Lawrence River and can be found year-round, often in large colonies, in southeastern Alaska, along the Pacific coast from southern British Columbia to northern California, in the Colorado River Delta and Gulf of California, along the Atlantic coast from Newfoundland to New York, and in all of Florida except the panhandle. Double-crested Cormorant populations and ranges seem to be expanding. You are likely to see the birds as they swim low in the water, their snaky necks and up-tilted bills the only parts visible above the surface, or as they loaf on sandbars, pilings, trees, and other perches, their wings outstretched to dry in the sunshine.

Their name refers to nuptial crests that grow on each side of the bird's head during breeding season, March through May. The crests may be either black or white. Far more useful as a field mark is the bare skin of the throat pouch at the base of their bill. It is bright orange and bordered by black feathers.

LOOK FOR a dark, slender body; hooked bill; and bright orange throat pouch.

adult

Purple Gallinule

Porphyrio martinica

Purple Gallinules can be found during the summer along the Gulf and Atlantic coasts north to South Carolina and up the Mississippi River valley to southeastern Arkansas. They reside year-round in peninsular Florida, coastal Mexico, and the Greater Antilles east to Puerto Rico.

They are about the size and shape of the Common Moorhen, which also nests along the Gulf and Atlantic coasts. Both birds prefer marshes, and both have unusual yellow-tipped red bills that do not join their faces below and in front of the eyes, as on most birds, but instead extend up the forehead. These enlargements are known as frontal shields. They are pale blue on gallinules, red on moorhens.

Purple Gallinules are beautiful, colorful birds. Their heads, necks, and breasts are glossy bluish purple, the sides of their necks appear blue or green, and their backs are olive and iridescent. The feathers under their tails are entirely white. Like Common Moorhens, they have yellow legs and enormous feet. Watch for the feet as the birds tiptoe gingerly on top of floating plants.

Leg color, combined with the color of their frontal shields, will help you distinguish the gallinules from similar-looking exotic Purple Swamphens *(Porphyrio porphyrio)* in Florida. The swamphens were first noticed in Broward County in 1996 and are now breeding throughout southern Florida. They have large red frontal shields and pinkish legs, and their bills lack a yellow tip.

LOOK FOR iridescent purple and blue plumage, white feathers under the tail, a red bill with a yellow tip, and a blue frontal shield.

adult

Common Moorhen

Gallinula chloropus

adult

Common Moorhens can be found during the summer at scattered locations in the center of the United States and as far north as southeastern Ontario and extreme southern Quebec in the Great Lakes region. They reside year-round in wetlands throughout the West, in southern Texas, and along the Gulf and Atlantic coasts north to Virginia.

Moorhens are about the size and shape of the Purple Gallinule, a colorful rail that also nests along the Gulf and Atlantic coasts. Both birds prefer marshes, and both have unusual yellow-tipped red bills that do not join their faces below and in front of the eyes as on most birds but instead extend up the forehead. This frontal shield is red on moorhens (bright on breeding birds, dull on others) and pale blue on gallinules.

Common Moorhens have enormous feet and bright red patches at the top of their yellow legs. Their plumage is dark overall. Their heads and necks are blackish gray, their breasts and sides are dark blue-gray, and their wings and rump are olive-brown. Triangular white patches appear on either side of black feathers under the tail, and white markings on the flank feathers align to create a noticeable, and unique, stripe that runs along each side of the body. Neither the Purple Gallinule nor the American Coot has a stripe.

LOOK FOR a white stripe along the body, white feathers under the tail, a red bill with a yellow tip, and a red frontal shield.

American Coot

Fulica americana

American Coots are the most abundant species of rail in North America. From May through August, they can be heard cackling and grunting on vegetated freshwater ponds and marshes throughout the continent, especially in the prairie-pothole region of southern Canada and the north-central United States. In winter months, they can be found swimming, their heads bobbing back and forth as they go, in waters along the Atlantic coast, in the lower Mississippi River valley, along the Gulf coast of Texas and Louisiana, and in California's Central Valley. They breed in Central America from Mexico south to northwestern Costa Rica and in South America from Colombia south to northwestern Argentina.

Coots share the shape and are about the size of a Common Moorhen or Purple Gallinule but lack these birds' red bills and blue and green coloration. Rather, they are covered front to back in dark slate-gray feathers. Their black heads and necks are even darker. Small triangular patches of white feathers under their tails are useful field marks, as are their stubby white bills. Look for a dark band near their tip and a reddish brown or white callus on the forehead above the upper mandible. And if you are lucky enough to come across a coot walking on dry or mucky land, be sure to look at its feet. Its toes are lobed and comically long.

LOOK FOR a slate-gray bird with white feathers under the tail, stubby white bill, and oversize feet with lobed toes.

adult

4

GEESE

Geese are in the same taxonomic family as ducks but are usually larger and have distinctive characteristics. They are, for the most part, social birds that gather in large, sometimes enormous, flocks. They honk and trumpet loudly. Unlike ducks, geese often bond in pairs for life. Geese are much better adapted for walking than are many ducks; their legs are well centered beneath their bodies, allowing them to walk comfortably on dry land, where some species spend long hours grazing.

Barnacle Goose

Branta leucopsis

adults

Barnacle Geese are only visitors to North America, and rare ones at that. They breed in eastern Greenland, on the arctic island of Spitsbergen north of Norway, and on the archipelago of Novaya Zemlya north of Russia. The birds build their nests on high cliffs from which their hungry, fuzz-covered goslings leap, spectacularly, when they are only days old. Almost all of the species' infrequent appearances on this continent have been in the East.

Male Barnacle Geese are larger than females; otherwise the sexes wear the same high-contrast plumage. Their faces are creamy white; their breasts, necks, and crowns are solid black; and their sides and flanks are whitish gray. The boundary of each of these areas is a crisp line. The border of the face patch starts on the throat and curls around the cheeks and over the forehead; the dark feathers of the chest terminate in a sharp line that loops from shoulder to shoulder across the lower breast. The abrupt contrast between the dark breast and the white belly, undertail coverts, and rump makes an excellent field mark on flying Barnacle Geese.

Up close, look for subtle gray barring on the pale flanks. White-edged, brownish black feathers on the upper back and gray wing feathers tipped with black-and-white bands combine to create much bolder barring on the goose's upper half.

LOOK FOR whitish gray sides and flanks, barred back, black breast and neck, and a white face.

Canada Goose

Branta canadensis

The Canada Goose is North America's signature goose. It can be found just about anywhere on the continent at some time of the year—across much of the United States, it can be found year-round. Its rising, two-syllable, honking voice is a familiar backdrop to outdoor activities, even in urban areas. Canada Geese, like other geese, fly in noisy V-shaped flocks. A combination of its shape and its autumnal brown, black, and white coloration is what most people imagine when they think "goose."

Male Canada Geese are larger than females; otherwise, the sexes look alike. All have black tails, black legs and bills, and heads and necks that look as if a long, black stocking has been pulled down over them. The feathers under their tails are white, and a band of white, the species' best-known field mark, extends up from the chin to behind each eye. Their backs, wings, flanks, and sides can be called brownish, but actual colors vary across the continent from dark chocolate or slatey-brown to pale gray-brown. Size also varies, and dramatically. The Giant Canada Goose, the largest subspecies, weighs almost eleven pounds; the smallest, known as Lesser Canada Goose, weighs just over seven pounds.

Distinguishing a small Canada Goose from a Cackling Goose, a tundra species split from the Canada Goose complex in 2004, requires making careful judgments about size and shape. Cackling Geese are tiny (the average weight of the smallest subspecies is just over three pounds), and they have short necks, round heads, and stubby bills. As its name suggests, the Cackling Goose makes a squeaky, high-pitched cackle, not a honk.

LOOK FOR brownish breast, sides, and back; black head and neck; and a white patch on each side of the face.

adult with chick

Brant

Branta bernicla

adult

Brant are small geese with short necks and small bills. Their heads, necks, and upper breasts are jet-black. Their upper tail coverts and rumps are white. Swimming birds look brighter when viewed from the rear than they do from the front. A garland of white feathers adorns their upper neck.

Their bellies, sides, and flanks vary in color from dark gray (almost black) to light gray, but you are unlikely to see much variation in any one flock. That's because the Brant that appear along the Pacific and Atlantic coasts of the United States and Mexico each winter belong to discrete populations that make long migrations to widely separated wintering grounds.

The Brant that visit the shallow bays and marshes along the Pacific coast, primarily in Mexico, have the darkest bellies. They breed in north-eastern Russia, along the west and north coasts of Alaska, and in the western and central low Arctic. Brant seen in Puget Sound, Washington, have lighter but still dark bellies; they breed on Melville and other west-ern high-Arctic islands. Brant observed along the East coast between Massachusetts and North Carolina are the lightest. They breed in the low Arctic, around the Foxe Basin.

LOOK FOR a black head, neck, and upper breast; white tail coverts and rump; and a garland of white on the upper neck.

Greater White-fronted Goose

Anser albifrons

The Greater White-fronted Goose is the only New World representative of a family of geese known in the Old World as "gray geese." Each year, between May and August, it breeds on open tundra from the Bering Sea to the western shore of Hudson Bay. Then it undertakes a monumental migration to spend the winter either west of the Rockies from British Columbia to western Mexico or in southeastern Arkansas and Texas, Louisiana, and central and eastern Mexico.

Male Greater White-fronted Geese are larger than females; otherwise the sexes look alike. Both have relatively short, dark necks and are brownish gray above and grayish below. Clean white feathers show above and especially beneath the tail. Irregular black patches cross the belly. Look for a white blaze on the forehead (inspiration for the goose's name), a pinkish orange bill, conspicuous bright orange legs, and, on each side of the body, a prominent white streak. The stripe is unique among North American geese. It is formed by the light-colored tips of the flank feathers.

Greater White-fronted Geese are more vocal in the air than on the ground. Their call is higher-pitched and more hurried than the one given by Greylag Geese. Flying Greater White-fronted Geese show two-toned upper wings. Look for a row of gray feathers just ahead of the dark feathers along the trailing edge.

LOOK FOR black marks on the belly, white blaze on the forehead, pinkish orange bill, orange legs, and a prominent white lateral streak.

adult

TONY MERCIECA

Greylag Goose

Anser anser

Wild Greylag Geese do not breed in North America, but in Iceland, Scandinavia, and Finland and from southeastern Europe across Asia to China. Members of a western subspecies winter in Great Britain; eastern greylags spend the winter in India, Burma, and China. The species is the ancestor of most of our domesticated barnyard geese, however, and feral greylags are seen on occasion in flocks of Canada Geese, so it pays to be on the lookout for them.

Greylags are big, bulky geese with large heads. Like white-fronted geese, they are generally brownish gray above and grayish below. The feathers immediately above and below their tails are white. But they lack the other goose's white blaze on the forehead and its characteristic black patches on the belly. Greylags' legs are pink, not orange. Moreover, their bills are noticeably thick at the base, making them look more triangular than those on white-fronteds. Greylags' head, neck, breast, belly, rump, and tail are conspicuously pale, as are the underwing linings and the leading edges of their upper wings. These field marks are especially apparent when the birds fly. Their call is a loud, nasal cackling.

LOOK FOR a bulky goose with pink legs and a big head with a thick-based, triangular bill.

adult

Emperor Goose

Chen canagica

adult

Only very small numbers of Emperor Geese are seen each winter as far south as Washington, Oregon, or northern California. The majority gathers on the beaches of the Alaska Peninsula and farther west on the Aleutian Islands, not far from the flat tidal marshes of western Alaska and coastal Russia, where they breed. They are creatures of the Bering Sea.

Emperors are small geese, about the size of Brant, but appear stockier. Adults of both sexes have small, pinkish bills and orange legs and are simply marked and eye-catching. Blue-gray feathers cover their bodies and the fronts of their necks; their heads and the backs of their necks are white. The two colors meet in a neat, gently curving line that runs from the shoulder to the chin, dividing the neck into a white back and black front. The individual feathers that cover the body are marked with black bands and white tips. Arranged side by side, the feathers create a handsome barred pattern on the goose's back and a scalloped pattern on its belly and breast.

Emperors' tails are white, but the feathers that cover the base of the tail are dark. When the geese fan their tails, look for a broad, white U-shape. And pay attention to the feathers under the tail—unique among adult North American geese, they are dark, not white.

LOOK FOR a blue-gray body, orange legs, white head, and a neck that is black in front and white in the back.

Snow Goose

Chen caerulescens

white adult

Adult Snow Geese are North America's grinning geese. They have wedge-shaped, rose-pink bills whose upper and lower parts don't meet in a straight line but pull away from each other instead. The gap exposed is black and often called a grin patch. It's a valuable field mark, useful for distinguishing Snow Geese from Ross's Geese, which look nearly identical but are smaller and have no grin patch.

Snow Geese breed in large colonies near the top of the world from northeastern Russia across arctic and subarctic Canada to western Greenland. They winter in locations across the United States and Mexico. Their annual flights in loud, huge, V-shaped flocks—to primary winter destinations in Delaware Bay, the Central Valley of California, and along the Missouri River and Gulf coast of Texas and Louisiana—are some of the greatest wildlife spectacles you will ever witness.

All adult Snow Geese have dark pink legs and feet, and most are almost completely white. Only the primaries, the flight feathers closest to the tip of each wing, are black. A certain type, or morph, of Snow Geese, especially those that winter along the Gulf coast and in the Mississippi Valley, are not entirely white, however. Known as blue geese (and until 1983 considered a separate species), they have white heads and white feathers on their necks and under the tail, but elsewhere they are black-brown. Feathers all along the trailing edge of each wing are black. They contrast sharply with the goose's white wing linings.

LOOK FOR a white goose with black-tipped, white wings and a grin patch—or a black-brown goose with a white head and a grin patch.

dark adult

Ross's Goose

Chen rossii

Ross's Geese build their nests on Southampton and Baffin Islands and along the western and southern shores of Hudson Bay, but the great majority—ninety-five percent of the world population—breeds in the cold tundra marshes that line Queen Maud Gulf in Nunavut, in the central Canadian Arctic. Most Ross's Geese later migrate to the Central Valley of California, but you will also find overwintering geese in New Mexico, the central highlands of Mexico, along the Gulf coast of Texas and Louisiana, and on the Atlantic coast—often in flocks of Snow Geese.

Their choice of company can complicate identification because Ross's Geese and white-morph Snow Geese are nearly identical. Both are almost completely white. Only the very tips of their wings are black. And both have pink bills and dark pink legs and feet. At a glance, you could easily mistake one for the other.

But the overall size and shape of the Ross's Goose are important field marks. The Ross's is a noticeably smaller goose. Its average body mass is two-thirds that of the Snow Goose. Its neck is shorter, and its head is rounder. Moreover, its bill is small and stubby. The line formed where it meets the face is not concave, as it is on Snow Geese, but straight. Most important, the bill lacks a grin patch.

LOOK FOR a white goose with a black-tipped white wings and a stubby bill.

adult

TONY MERCIECA

INDEX OF SPECIES